CONTENTS

Yesterday was a bad day. Devin spent English class with a spitball in his hair. Kyle had been using him for "target practice" for weeks. It was **humiliating**. What made it even more embarrassing was that none of the kids in the class told Devin the spitball was there or stuck up for him. Some even laughed. But Devin knew that it was only going to get worse—Kyle told him that he needed to "watch his back" tomorrow.

For most of that night, Devin was awake worrying about what Kyle meant. Devin considered telling his mom that he was sick, but he didn't want to upset her. Last year, he had so many "sick" days that he had gotten behind; going from straight A's to a report card dotted with C's and D's.

When Devin went to school the next morning, his heart started racing. Even the building made him nervous. In math class, the numbers blurred on the page. By recess, he just wanted to get it over with. Kyle was waiting for him in the playground. "Walk with me, Freak," Kyle whispered.

Devin thought about running or telling, but didn't want to make things worse. He followed Kyle behind the trees, where they were out of the teachers' sight. "Now, turn around," said Kyle.

Devin did. He felt the pain instantly. Kyle had kicked him—hard—at the back of his knee, knocking him down. A crowd of Kyle's friends had gathered. They were enjoying the show. "Now, eat dirt and I'll let you go...for today," sneered Kyle.

Devin imagined getting up and slapping Kyle's face, but he was just one and Kyle had his group. Instead, Devin picked up the dirt, closed his eyes and slowly put it in his mouth.

Take A Stand Against Bullying
PHYSICAL BULLYING

Jennifer Rivkin

Crabtree Publishing Company
www.crabtreebooks.com

TAKE A STAND AGAINST BULLYING

Author: Jennifer Rivkin

Publishing plan research and development:
Sean Charlebois, Reagan Miller
Crabtree Publishing Company

Project coordinator: Kathy Middleton

Editorial director: Melissa McClellan

Art director: Tibor Choleva

Fictional Introductions: Jennifer Rivkin

Editors: Kristine Thornley, Molly Aloian

Proofreader: Kelly McNiven

Production coordinator: Margaret Amy Salter

Prepress technician: Margaret Amy Salter

Print coordinator: Katherine Berti

Developed and produced by: BlueApple*Works* Inc.

Consultants:
Adina Herbert, MSW, RSW
Social Worker, Youth Addictions and Concurrent Disorders Service
Centre for Addiction and Mental Health, Toronto, ON, Canada

Lesley Cunningham MSW, RSW
Social Worker - Violence Prevention

Photographs: Front cover: Shutterstock (left), Thinkstock (right); Title page: ©pjcross/ Shutterstock Inc.; Contents page, p.17 © Creatista/ Shutterstock Inc.; p. 4, 41 © Leah-Anne Thompson/ Shutterstock Inc.; p. 6 © Helder Almeida/ Shutterstock Inc.; p. 7 © Andrey Shadrin/ Shutterstock Inc.; p. 8 © Molly Klager; p. 10 © prudkov/ Shutterstock Inc.; p. 11 © Dmitry Sagalaev/ Shutterstock Inc.; p. 12 © Galina Barskaya/ Shutterstock Inc.; p. 14 © XXX/ Shutterstock Inc.; p. 15 p. © oliveromg/ Shutterstock Inc.; p. 16, 20 © Monkey Business Images/ Shutterstock Inc.; p. 18 ©Vladimir Wrangel/ Shutterstock Inc.; p. 19 © Stuart Monk/ Shutterstock Inc.; p. 21 © @erics/ Shutterstock Inc.; p. 22 © Amy Myers/ Shutterstock Inc.; p. 23 © Molly Klager; p. 24 © Alexander Gitlits/ Shutterstock Inc.; p. 25 © Elena Rostunova/ Shutterstock Inc.; p. 26 Featureflash/ Shutterstock Inc.; p. 27 © netbritish/ Shutterstock Inc.; p. 28, 32 © Tad Denson/ Shutterstock Inc.; p. 29 © chert28/ Shutterstock Inc.; p. 30 © Mandy Godbehear/ Shutterstock Inc.;p. 30 © Sascha Burkard / Shutterstock Inc.; p. 33 © Konstantin Sutyagin/ Shutterstock Inc.; p. 34 © rui vale sousa/ Shutterstock Inc.; p. 35 © Alexander Raths/ Shutterstock Inc.; p. 36 © Pshek/ Shutterstock Inc.; p. 38 © Tracy Whiteside/ Shutterstock Inc.; p. 39 © Tom Prokop/ Shutterstock Inc.; p. 40 © Lisa F. Young/ Shutterstock Inc.; p.45 © Peter Close; p. 42 © auremar / Shutterstock Inc.; torn paper background © LeksusTuss; banners: © Amgun/ Shutterstock Inc.

Library and Archives Canada Cataloguing in Publication

Rivkin, Jennifer
    Physical bullying / Jennifer Rivkin.

(Take a stand against bullying)
Includes index.
Issued also in electronic format.
ISBN 978-0-7787-7914-8 (bound).--ISBN 978-0-7787-7919-3 (pbk.)

    1. Bullying--Juvenile literature. I. Title. II. Series: Take a stand against bullying

BF637.B85R58 2013   j302.34'3   C2013-900250-2

Library of Congress Cataloging-in-Publication Data

Rivkin, Jennifer.
  Physical bullying / Jennifer Rivkin.
    pages cm. -- (Take a stand against bullying)
  Includes index.
  ISBN 978-0-7787-7914-8 (reinforced library binding) -- ISBN 978-0-7787-7919-3 (pbk.) -- ISBN 978-1-4271-9075-8 (electronic pdf) -- ISBN 978-1-4271-9129-8 (electronic html)
  1. Aggressiveness in children--Juvenile literature. 2. Violence in children--Juvenile literature. 3. Bullying--Prevention--Juvenile literature. I. Title.

  BF723.A35R59 2013
  302.34'3--dc23
             2013000562

Crabtree Publishing Company
www.crabtreebooks.com   1-800-387-7650

Printed in Canada/022013/BF20130114

Published in Canada
Crabtree Publishing
616 Welland Ave.
St. Catharines, ON
L2M 5V6

Published in the United States
Crabtree Publishing
PMB 59051
350 Fifth Avenue, 59th Floor
New York, NY 10118

Published in the United Kingdom
Crabtree Publishing
Maritime House
Basin Road North, Hove
BN41 1WR

Published in Australia
Crabtree Publishing
3 Charles Street
Coburg North
VIC, 3058

The Nature of Physical Bullying

Kyle is using his body to **intimidate** Devin and cause him pain. This is an act of bullying: intentional, repeated, **aggressive** behavior intended to hurt, scare, and gain power over a victim.

Physical bullying is a huge problem in schools. While **cyber bullying** seems to be on everybody's minds these days, making headlines on TV and in the newspapers, the rise of online bullying doesn't mean that physical aggression has disappeared (or that it's any less hurtful). In fact, each of the four types of bullying—verbal, social, cyber, and physical— can be damaging in its own way.

In this book, you will learn what physical bullying is and what the consequences are. You will discover that even though bullying has been going on forever, it does not have to continue. Whether you are a bully, victim, or **bystander**, you can help put an end to bullying. How? Read on.

TAKE A STAND AGAINST

STOP

BULLYING

"There's a kid at school who won't leave me alone. I have no idea what I did to him to make him hate me. Every chance he gets, he tries to hurt me. He grabs my hands and pushes my fingers back or twists my arm behind my back until I say "mercy." Then he laughs. It's so embarrassing. I want to hurt him back." Eli, age 13

CHAPTER 1
What is Physical Bullying?

Physical bullying is using—or threatening to use—aggressive physical contact, such as hitting or kicking, to hurt, intimidate, or control another person. There are all kinds of physical bullying, including stealing someone's lunch money, locking someone in a bathroom stall or locker, or simply holding someone down on the ground.

Many people believe that physical bullying is easier to spot than social bullying, but that is not always true. It's sometimes hard to tell the difference between bullying and horseplay. Kids often roughhouse with friends by giving each other noogies or playing keep away with someone's hat. This is not an ideal way to behave at school, but it's not necessarily physical bullying.

Horseplay or Bullying?

The difference between horseplay and bullying is the relationship between the people involved. When the participants are friends and equals it may be considered horseplay. But when one person is exerting power over the other, either socially (because he or she is more popular) or physically (because he or she is stronger), it is bullying. Horseplay and bullying also differ in intent. During roughhousing, both people are playing and having fun. They are not really trying to hurt one another. When the goal is to hurt the other person, it is physical bullying.

Beware

Roughhousing can get out of control (which is why it's not a great idea in the first place) and can turn into physical bullying. If you can't get the other person to stop, if the physical contact is constant, or if the aggressor is trying to intimidate you, it is no longer fun.

The physical bully seeks and maintains power through aggressive actions. The violence in physical bullying often gets worse over time.

How Common Is It?

If you have been bullied or witnessed someone else who has, you are not alone. In fact, one out of every four children reports being bullied—this means that millions of children are bullied each year. Studies show that by the time you graduate from high school, each of you will have been exposed to bullying, either directly or as a witness.

Boys are more likely to be physical bullies and the targets of physical bullying than girls, but research indicates that girls are increasingly turning to physical aggression.

? Did You Know?

The frequency of physical bullying peaks between grades 6 and 8 and then declines gradually.

Physical bullying is more likely to occur during certain years of your life. The amount of physical bullying increases through elementary school, peaks between grades 6 and 8, and then gradually declines. Perhaps this is because as children enter adolescence, they naturally have a desire to be accepted and be part of the group. **Peer pressure** is intense, and social hierarchies are formed during these years. Kids who want to be at the top of the social ladder might turn to bullying, and those who don't "fit in" can become the victims.

As you get older, the likelihood of physical bullying decreases, but, unfortunately, it never goes away entirely. Even adults can be physical bullies. It's very likely that adults who use their size and strength to hurt others started out as bullies when they were young. Bullying is not something that happens out of the blue. That's why it's so important to learn what you can do to stop the cycle now.

Who Is Involved?

People can play different roles during acts of physical bullying:

Bully: The perpetrator of the **assault**.

Target: The person on the receiving end of the attack.

Bystander(s): A person or group of people who witnesses the bullying.

Ally(ies): A person or group of people who steps in to help the victim.

Most people have played one of these roles at some point.

Where Can Physical Bullying Happen?

Not all bullying takes place at school. A bully can be in your neighborhood, at an extra-curricular activity, on the bus, or on your sports team. The locker room can be a breeding ground for physical aggression. Players who are weaker and believed to be bringing the team down or players who are doing well and getting attention from the coach could be possible **targets**. Bullies may try to intimidate targets with violence, such as tripping or shoving.

Siblings Acting Like Bullies

A bully may be in your own house. Older siblings are usually bigger and stronger, so the home is a common place for physical bullying to occur. If your brother or sister is hurting or **restraining** you, or threatening to beat you up if you don't do what he or she asks, you are being bullied. If this happens to you, you should talk to your parents about it.

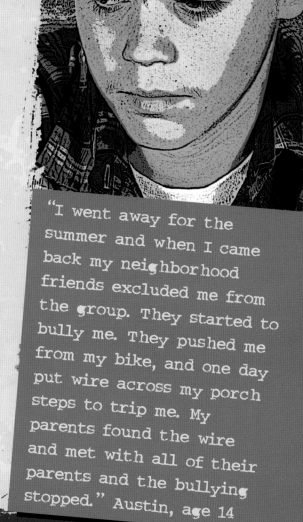

? Did You Know?

Approximately 15 percent of students ages 11 to 15 are involved in weekly physical bullying.

Parents Can Be Bullies Too!

But what if it's the adults in the house who are the physical bullies? If your parents are using violence or threatening you with violence, you need help. Tell another adult you can trust or use a resource like the Boys Town National Hotline or the Kids Help Phone—they can help you 24 hours a day.

"I went away for the summer and when I came back my neighborhood friends excluded me from the group. They started to bully me. They pushed me from my bike, and one day put wire across my porch steps to trip me. My parents found the wire and met with all of their parents and the bullying stopped." Austin, age 14

! Think About It!

Have you ever been physically bullied? How did it feel?
Have you ever bullied someone else? Why did you do it?
Have you ever seen someone get bullied at school or elsewhere? What did you do?

"I was bullied by my brother who is two years older than me. He would tackle me and hold me down for hours while my parents were out. He beat me up so badly that I needed stitches twice. He also destroyed things in my room. It was an every day thing. I became so quiet that the kids at school picked on me too. All I thought about was getting through the day." Jasmine, age 13

A Character Builder?

Certain people believe that bullying builds character, but this is not true. Bullying actually tears a person down. Over time, people who are bullied lose trust in others and in themselves.

As negative emotions such as fear, shame, and anger build up, some victims react outwardly, exploding in violent retaliation. Other victims may react inwardly, harming themselves by drinking, doing drugs, or cutting themselves. Unfortunately, children have even taken their own lives because of bullying.

Bullying has serious and lasting consequences and should not be tolerated. The first step is speaking up about the problem.

! Think About It!

How do you think being physically attacked makes a person feel? What feels worse, physical pain or emotional pain? Why?

"In my last year of middle school, there was a group of kids that tried to take me down at recess. I was too embarrassed to tell a teacher. I hid in the bathroom whenever I could. Eventually, I had to go out. When I did, the kids would find me and start kicking me. I switched schools, but I couldn't get away from bullying. By high school, I had no self esteem left." Will, age 20

CHAPTER 3

Physical Bullying Behaviors

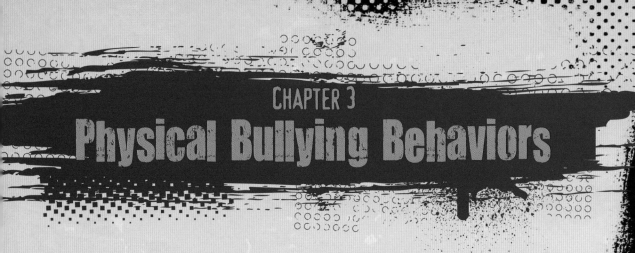

Direct Contact Physical Assault

"Use your words" and "Keep your hands to yourself" are some of the first lessons that parents and educators try to teach kids. Step into a preschool class and you'll hear those phrases repeated over and over as some of the kids bite, pinch, or shove each other to get the best toy or spot on the circle-time carpet. Young kids do this because they haven't developed patience or the language skills to ask for what they want. Older bullies also use aggressive physical contact (shoving, punching, and anything in between) to get what they want. What they want is power over the victim.

Indirect Contact

Even acts that don't involve directly touching a victim can be classified as physical bullying. For example, spitting on someone or dumping the contents of a person's lunch fall into this category.

Hazing

Some groups require new members to take part in hazing rituals. Those being hazed are expected to engage in dangerous, humiliating—and sometimes illegal—activities before being accepted into the group. There have been a number of hazing incidents at elementary schools and even more at high schools, but hazing rituals are most often used by sports teams, social clubs like fraternities, and the military. In sports, for example, when new athletes join a team, they may get towel-slapped by all of the current team members or be told to run naked across the field or through the gym.

At the extreme end of hazing, being "jumped in" to a gang may involve being beaten by other gang members, assaulting an innocent person, or shoplifting.

According to those doing the hazing, it's all in the name of group bonding. But, these types of customs, which are often kept secret, can easily get out of control and cause pain and humiliation to the new recruits.

Hazing is similar to bullying in that it is a way for the aggressors to show and maintain power over the target. The target is treated as "lesser than" or undeserving of the same treatment as the bully.

Some people believe that hazing is just another form of bullying and not a separate act at all.

"My bullies always acted so perfect at school when they were in front of the teachers. As soon as we were walking home, they would start with me. They would walk behind me and take turns throwing clumps of dirt at my head. Eventually, I came up with excuses to stay late after school." Hannah, age 13

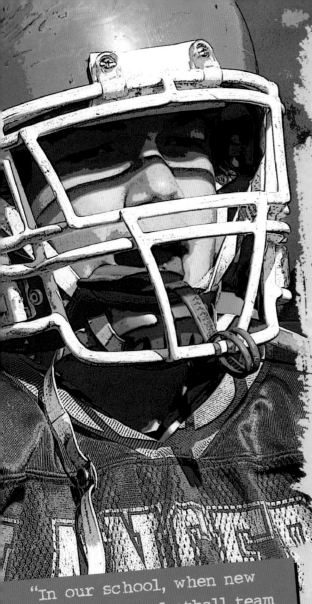

Why Is Hazing "Okay"?

So, if it's bullying, why is it allowed to continue? Many hazing incidents are not reported because the targets think it's okay, they do not want to be excluded by the group, or they are ashamed of the activities they took part in.

These rituals should not be considered harmless pranks. Many times, participants are threatened into being hazed. In addition, the physical abuse in these rituals can put kids in immediate danger and the emotional effects of the embarrassment can last a long time.

"In our school, when new kids join the football team they have to face 'the wall.' All the rookies have to bend over while the older boys throw the balls as hard as they can at them."
Andrew, age 16

? Did You Know?

In elementary and middle schools, almost one third of all bullying is physical. Boys are more likely to engage in physical bullying than girls.

Forced Confinement

Shoving kids into lockers or garbage cans is a classic move for television bullies. It may seem funny when it happens on TV shows, but in real life it's no laughing matter. Sometimes, physical bullies will restrain their victims by holding them down, putting them in a headlock, or locking them into a room. Can you imagine how frustrated and helpless this would make you feel?

Think About It!

Do you think that hazing is any different from bullying? Why or why not?

"I have been bullied at school because I am different. I have been kicked, hit, and shoved. Kids have hurt me with their words. I have been bullied and it is not okay." Janelle, age 12

CHAPTER 4
Understanding the Target

Being pushed once by an aggressive person doesn't necessarily lead to a pattern of abuse. There are some characteristics that can make a person more likely to be bullied.

Anyone can be a victim of bullying, but many targets of physical bullying are shyer and less **assertive** than their peers. They can be described as passive victims because they don't provoke their bully, or defend themselves. Passive victims don't report incidents of bullying—instead they may cry or back away. Unfortunately, this may strengthen a bully's feeling of power, which is what he or she is seeking.

Physical bullies don't generally choose victims who are likely to retaliate—they choose people that they think will be easy targets. Bullies look for kids who are physically weaker and unable or unwilling to fight back or who don't have friends that will **intervene**. Bullies don't look for a fair fight.

Some Celebrities Were Bullied Too!

If you are being bullied, you are in good company. Many famous people have gone through it, too. These celebs have gotten the best revenge—success! Now, they are speaking out about their own experiences to help others.

Comedian Chris Rock, who is African American, was beaten up and verbally attacked with **racial slurs** when he was in school. He developed a sitcom, *Everybody Hates Chris*, based on his real experiences.

In school, pop sensation and actress Miley Cyrus was tormented by a group that called themselves the "Anti-Miley Club." Her bullies once locked her in a bathroom during class.

Twilight's Robert Pattinson is popular now, but he was often beaten up when he was younger.

During his school years, actor Tom Cruise was an easy target. He was smaller than the other kids, had dyslexia, and moved a lot so he was often the new kid.

Who Is the Target?

Physical bullies may also select targets who are perceived to be on a lower rung of the social ladder or who stand out in some way. They pick on people they don't think fit in. For example, targets may be of a different race, religion, or **sexual orientation**. Targets may dress differently, either because they want to express themselves or because they can't afford the trends of the moment. They may have physical features that stand out, for example, being short, tall, overweight, or skinny. Also, kids who don't fit **gender stereotypes** or who have physical or intellectual disabilities are often targeted.

"I used to be bullied all the time, but I finally spoke up and it stopped."
Ryan, age 13

Think About It!

Who are the people that are physically bullied in your school? What do they have in common with each other? Why do you think the bully has selected them as targets? If the victims could change something about themselves to be less of a target, do you think they should try? Why or why not?

"Basically, I picked on people because I could. I was more popular and I knew they were scared of me. At the time, it felt good." Tyler, age 15

CHAPTER 5

Understanding the Bully

Just like their victims, bullies come in all shapes and sizes and from all backgrounds. However, physical bullies are more likely to be boys—they tend to use their size and strength to intimidate. Girls tend to use more social forms of bullying like gossip and exclusion in order to maintain popularity. However, over the past several decades the difference between boys and girls in terms of bullying behavior is becoming less clear. Girls are more likely to be physical bullies than ever before—not the type of gender equality we are striving for!

There is a myth that all bullies are angry, have problems at home, or difficulties at school. It's true that some children who physically bully come from homes with conflict— they may be abused by their parents or siblings or may have seen a parent being beaten. Many bullies have not learned how to deal with conflict properly.

Who Is the Bully?

Some bullies are also impulsive and have low self-esteem. This type of bully tends to be jealous, lose his or her temper quickly, and mistake others' common actions for hostility. For example, they may think someone is disrespecting them when the person is actually making an innocent comment. Bullies also lack **empathy** for others and dislike authority and rules. Many physical bullies have used aggression from a young age, get frustrated easily, and think of violence in a positive way—for example they enjoy violent video games, and violence on TV. Some have been bullied in the past and try to feel better by demeaning others. But, while these characteristics are true for some, new research shows that less than half of bullies fit this profile.

? Did You Know?

Children who observe adults ignoring bullying are at greater risk of becoming bullies.

Bullies often deny the behavior when they are caught.

Who Is Most at Risk?

Physical bullies generally select targets who:

- are smaller, weaker, or younger
- are less popular
- have few friends to back them up
- are new in school
- have mental or physical disabilities
- are sensitive or anxious (cry or back away when confronted)
- are shy or have low self-confidence
- are labelled "too smart or talented" (kids who get top grades or kids who are great in sports)
- are labeled "not smart or talented enough"
- belong to a racial or ethnic minority
- belong to a religious minority
- are economically disadvantaged
- are gay, lesbian, bisexual, or **transgendered** (LGBT) or are perceived to be LGBT
- don't fit gender stereotypes (boys who are labelled "sensitive" or "creative" or girls who are "tomboys")
- look "different" (e.g., are overweight, have acne, don't wear the latest fashions)
- are socially or physically awkward
- engage in behaviors that others find irritating

Important note: There are certainly some traits that can make a person more likely to be a target of physical bullying, but it is never the victim's fault. Most people are different in some way. Many of these characteristics can't be changed, and even if they could, doing so would only be giving the bully the power that they want.

Bully in Disguise

So, what about the majority? You may be surprised to know that most bullies have high self-esteem and good social skills, are popular, do well in school, get along with adults, and are generally happy. But anyone is capable of being a bully. Some people who are considered bullies may not even be aware that others view them that way. Sometimes, members of a dominant group in society feel that it's okay to treat others poorly. Bullies may be prejudiced against other groups and bullying can be motivated by things like **classism**, racism, or **homophobia**.

Bullies are not all alike in their characters, but their motivations are the same—they are seeking power over others. Some do this because they believe that it will protect them from being bullied themselves. Most bullies use aggression as a way to achieve and maintain the popularity that they feel they are entitled to.

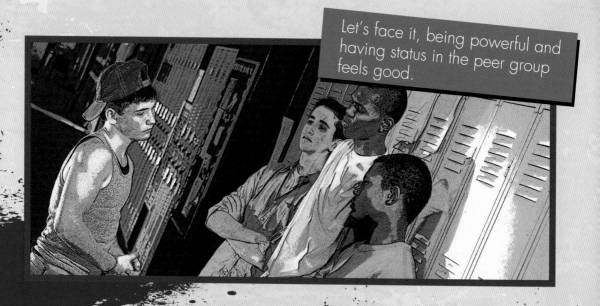

Let's face it, being powerful and having status in the peer group feels good.

Bullying Hurts...Everyone

You probably aren't surprised that bullying hurts victims. But did you know that bullies also harm themselves when they abuse others?

By acting out physically, bullies reinforce negative social interactions. They learn that they can use force and intimidate others to get what they want. Many bullies don't learn social skills like sharing and empathy. Making people scared of you doesn't build real friendships or respect. Most bullies eventually lose friends. As a result, bullies are generally popular in elementary school and become less popular in high school. Bullying is not a good long-term strategy for popularity. After all, who wants to be friends with someone who is mean or violent?

"I used to be a bully because I was bullied. I felt bad about myself and took it out on other people. I was awful. I have stopped, but I still feel so bad for the people I have hurt." Ashley, age 13

Grown-Up Bullies

If bullies continue to get away with their behavior—and get what they want out of it—they can become adults with anti-social behavior, drug and alcohol addiction, depression, and an increased risk of suicide. Continuing with this behavior into adulthood can lead to problems at work and with relationships. As adults, bullies may engage in domestic violence (spousal or child abuse). Bullying is a behavior that you should change so that it doesn't lead to problems in the future.

"I was a bully. I targeted these boys because they were easy. They were quiet and didn't stand up for themselves. I didn't think of myself as a bully until my good friend started getting depressed because he was being bullied. The boy was doing the same thing to him that I was doing to other people! That's when I knew I had to stop." Nicholas, age 16

? Did You Know?

Children who both bully and are victimized (bully-victims) may be at the greatest risk for physical health problems and other negative consequences associated with bullying.

Criminal Behavior

Bullying is taken very seriously in schools and can lead to serious punishment at school, at home, and with the police. In many schools, bullying can result in suspension or expulsion.

While bullying itself is not a crime, many of the behaviors associated with bullying are crimes. These include uttering threats, mischief (damaging or destroying property), theft, and assault. These offenses are punishable under the law and can result in criminal action that can affect your future.

The physical bully is the most likely to move on to serious criminal offenses as he or she gets older. One study found that 60 percent of boys who bully others in elementary school had criminal records by age 24.

Think About It!

Have you ever bullied someone? Why did you do it? Do you know someone who is a physical bully? What type of person are they? How do you think this behavior is affecting this person? What do you think could happen if he or she continues?

"I watched as my good friend, who was new to our school, got bullied. I didn't stop it because I wanted to stay part of the in crowd. Being a bystander and doing nothing to help is terrible. By not stepping in, I know that I was bullying my friend, too. I hate myself for it. If you see someone being bullied, you should definitely try to do something about it." Josh, age 15

CHAPTER 6
Bystanders Have Power

Most physical bullying takes place in front of other people. You may be surprised that witnesses have as big of an influence on the situation as bullies or targets. While bullies are seeking power through their actions, bystanders actually do have the power. Depending on what they do, bystanders can promote bullying or prevent it. It's not just kids that encourage the bully who do damage—kids who watch in silence hurt the victim as well. These bystanders are providing an audience and giving the bully attention that makes him or her feel important. These bystanders may not directly encourage bullies, but they help them get away with it by remaining silent.

When bullies see that no one will step in, they have no reason to stop, and may even think that the bystanders agree with their actions. Watching someone get physically abused and doing nothing is, in effect, saying it's okay. What makes it even worse is that the victim feels ganged up on. By doing nothing, the bystander becomes a bully, too.

Why Don't More Bystanders Step In?

When bystanders don't intervene, they often feel guilty, weak, and anxious afterward. Still, many remain silent because stepping in can be scary. Bystanders worry about the bully turning on them—they don't want to become the target themselves, lose their popularity, or be labelled as a rat.

Witnesses may also stand back because they don't know how to help or they don't realize the impact they can have on the situation. They may think, "There's nothing I can do," or "It's not my business." If you've read this far, you know better. You realize that you can do something and that bullying is everyone's problem.

Helpful Bystanders

Helpful bystanders to bullying are also called allies. Allies are those who step up to help the victim. They can help while the incident is happening by telling the bully to stop and encouraging other bystanders to do the same.

When you see somebody being bullied, step in and help the victim. It will boost your self-confidence.

Hurtful Bystanders

Some bystanders join forces with the bully and egg them on, either by laughing or by joining the assault against the victim. Hurtful bystanders do this because they have little empathy for the victim, they feel that he or she deserves it, they are friends with the bully, or they are bullies themselves. Other bystanders may not be as eager to join in, but take part because they want to be popular, get on the bully's good side—or stay off of his or her bad side.

? Did You Know?

Student bystanders are present in 85 percent of the bullying incidents at school. More than half of the time, bullying stops within 10 seconds of a bystander stepping in to help.

"I see people in my school get bullied for no other reason than that they are different. I am sick of being a bystander. From now on, I am going to speak up for the people that can't speak up for themselves." Alyssa, age 16

What to Do if You Witness Bullying

Think about how you would feel if you were the one being bullied. You would want someone in your corner, right? You can be that person.

? Did You Know?
Bullying incidents last longer when bystanders laugh or cheer on the bully.

In the case of physical bullying, the best option is to walk away and get an adult who can help immediately. You should never try to intervene directly if you think that there is a chance you could get hurt. When bystanders step into physical bullying situations, they tend to do so aggressively. Don't respond with violence; it will only make the situation worse.

If you feel safe doing so, tell the bully to stop. Don't sink to the bully's level by calling him or her names. A simple "Don't do that" or "That's not cool" is enough. Ask your fellow bystanders to help.

If it's not possible to get an adult right away, report the incident afterwards. Remember: as a community of students, you are each responsible for each others' well being.

The Role of the School

Your school's administration should not be bystanders to bullying either. They are responsible for providing you with a safe environment for learning. Presenting bullying awareness information in class and in assemblies is important. **Peer mediators** on the playground and in school can also be helpful. Research has shown that peer mediation can reduce physical aggression by 50 percent.

Putting an end to bullying must be a group effort. The school's focus should be on preventing bullying from happening in the first place. Many schools already have prevention programs in place. This means creating a culture where bullying is taken seriously and is not accepted. Your school should be an environment where there are quick and consistent consequences for bullying. It is also your school's obligation to make it simple for you to report incidents anonymously, such as using suggestion boxes.

! Think About It!

Have you ever seen someone being physically bullied? What did you do? What would you do now? Is your school doing enough to end bullying? What are your teachers and principals doing right? What do you think they could do better? Write these suggestions down and give them to your teacher. You can be part of the solution.

CHAPTER 7

Empower Yourself

People may have told you that it's best to ignore bullies, that everyone goes through it, and that there will always be bullying because there always has been. These are dangerous myths. Just because it has gone on before doesn't mean that it has to continue.

The reality is that you need to take action as soon as possible. Tell your teachers and your parents, or use other resources, such as websites and telephone hotlines that are set up to help you. Try to find someone to be with at lunch, recess, and walking home—there is strength in numbers. If the bullies still target you, stand up for yourself. Don't respond aggressively or give in. Instead, firmly but calmly say, "Leave me alone." Then, walk away if you can. If you can't, shout for help.

Think twice about joining any group or team where humiliation or pain is a requirement for becoming a member.

Tips for Being Assertive with Bullies

Be Assertive with Your Body Language: If you are slouching or have your head down, a bully may feel that you are an easy target. Stand up straight, keep your head high, and make eye contact with the bully.

Speak Up: Speak confidently and firmly and tell the bully that you will not be a victim. Use your own words to say something to the effect of "back off." Do what you can to send the message that you won't put up with it. Practice this at home or role-play with a friend, so that when the time comes, you are ready.

Don't Stoop to Their Level: Do not call bullies names or threaten them.

Report the Bullying: If you are being called names or being physically bullied, speak up. Remember that reporting bullying is not tattling. If you witness bullying, report it.

Become an Ally: If you have a friend who is bullying, talk privately to them and tell them that you think they should stop and why. If you have a friend or peer who is bullied, stand up for him or her as you would want someone to do for you.

Start a Program: If you don't have an anti-bullying program or group in your school, talk to your principal about starting one.

Look for Support: Find a support group in your community or online, it can give you strength to know that you are not alone.

Don't Give Up: You may have tried to get help before. If it didn't work, keep trying to have your voice heard. It may take some time, and you may have to try a few different tactics, but it can get better. The most important thing to remember is that physical bullying is wrong and must be stopped.

Are You a Physical Bully?

You may have gone too far with a game of keep away, or played a little too rough. Someone may have even been hurt or embarrassed. But are these unusual events, or could you be a bully? Think back on this school year and answer these questions:

1. Have you physically hurt someone on purpose (hit, slapped)?
2. Have you threatened to hurt someone?
3. Have you taken or damaged someone's belongings?
4. Have you been a part of a group or team that has hazed other kids?
5. Do you think that some people deserve to be hurt?
6. Have you been involved in roughhousing that you thought was "just playing around," but the other person kept telling you to stop?
7. Did you ever hurt someone more than you intended?
8. Do you pick on kids who are different from you (such as in race or appearance) or smaller than you?
9. Have you been physically bullied, and now you think it's okay to do it to others?
10. Do you use your size or strength to hurt or intimidate others?
11. Do you want people to be afraid of you?
12. Do you feel good or powerful when you hurt others?
13. Do you have trouble controlling your anger and do you lash out at others?

If you answered "yes" to any of these questions, and it has happened more than once, you could be a physical bully. That's the bad news. The good news is that you don't have to be one anymore.

If You're a Bully

If you recognize yourself as a bully, this book is as important for you as it is for victims. You may not have realized how much your bullying was hurting others—and yourself. It's not too late to stop. Bullying is a behavior and behaviors can be changed.

First, consider how you have made people feel, and make a list of reasons you should stop. Apologize to your victims, tell them it won't happen again, and mean what you say. Then, think about why you did it. Were you trying to feel better about yourself? Were you trying to be popular? These aren't excuses, but it helps to know that they are triggers for your bullying. Learn to stop it before it starts. For example, if your concern is popularity, think of positive ways to be popular. Being kind and funny can be more effective than using scare tactics.

Talk to an adult and ask them for advice on resolving conflicts. If your home life has been part of the problem, or your temper is an issue, you may consider speaking with a counsellor or using a resource like Kids Help Phone or the Boys Town National Hotline. Change can be difficult at first, but it will get easier.

Other Resources

If you are dealing with bullying—either as a target, bystander, or bully—you don't have to go through it alone. There is information out there and people who are waiting to help. Don't hesitate to reach out if you need them.

Books

Dear Bully: 70 Authors Tell Their Stories, edited by Megan Kelley Hall and Carrie Jones. (HarperTeen, 2011).
Your favorite writers, including R.L. Stine, share essays about their experiences as either a victim, bully, or bystander. There are some great lessons to be learned from the experiences of people who have gone before you.

Bullied: What Every Parent, Teacher and Kid Needs to Know About Ending the Cycle of Fear, by Carrie Goldman (HaperOne, 2012).
This book features personal stories as well as concrete tips to end bullying. Have a read, and then pass it along to your parents and teachers. Putting an end to bullying must be a joint effort.

Websites

PrevNet: Promoting Relationships, and Eliminating Violence
www.prevnet.ca
This website features useful resources and information for victims, bullies, and bystanders.

PACER National Bullying Prevention Center
www.pacer.org/bullying
This informative site has great stories, videos, and up-to-date resources to help prevent bullying. Empower yourself by joining PACER's Kids Against Bullying Organization and become part of the solution.

Pink Shirt Day

www.pinkshirtday.ca

Here, you can learn more about how anti-bullying campaigns draw attention to the problem, and get inspired to join or start one in your area.

Organizations, Hotlines and Helplines

Kids Help Phone (Canada) (1-800-668-6868)

www.kidshelpphone.ca

Professional counselors can answer your questions on-line or by phone with this free, confidential service. It's open 24/7, 365 days a year.

Boys Town National Hotline (United States) (1-800-448-3000)

www.yourlifeyourvoice.org

Professional counselors can answer your questions on-line or by phone with this free, confidential service. It's open 24/7, 365 days a year.

My Gay Straight Alliance (Canada) (www.mygsa.ca)

MGSA.ca is Canada's website for safer and inclusive schools for the lesbian, gay, bisexual, trans, queer, and questioning (LGBTQ) community.

The Trevor Project (United States) (866-4-U-TREVOR)

www.thetrevorproject.org

The Trevor Project provides crisis intervention and suicide prevention services to lesbian, gay, bisexual, transgender, and questioning youth.

National Suicide Prevention Lifeline (United States) (1-800-273-TALK)

www.suicidepreventionlifeline.org

If you are having suicidal thoughts, call or chat online with a counselor now. They care and are waiting to help you.

Stomp Out Bullying Help Line (United States) (855-790-4357)

www.stompoutbullying.org/livechat_portal.php

This Live Help Chat Line is free and confidential for kids over 13. The counselors have been trained to help victims of bullying.

Glossary

aggressive Ready or likely to attack or confront forcefully

ally A person who is on someone's side, a supporter

anonymous Not named or identified

assault A violent attack or a threat or attempt to inflict bodily harm

assertive Showing a confident personality or behavior

bystander A person who is present at an incident but does not take part

classism Prejudice or discrimination based on wealth

cyber bullying Using technology (email, texts, blogs, social networking sites) to intimidate a person, hurt their feelings, or damage their reputation

emotional scars Permanent change in someone's character as a result of emotional distress

empathy Understanding what another person is feeling; being able to put yourself in their shoes

gender stereotype An idea about the way men or women are supposed to act or dress

homophobia Thinking less of people who are gay or lesbian

humiliating Making someone feel intense embarrassment

intervene To get between (people fighting) in order to prevent/stop it

intimidate Frighten someone in order to make them do what you want

peer mediator The use of other students to help resolve conflicts between groups and individuals peacefully

peer pressure Social pressure to act or dress in a way that conforms with others' expectations

racial slurs A disrespectful name for a racial group

restraining To hold someone back from doing something

sexual orientation Identity based on whether a person is attracted to the same sex (gay, lesbian), the opposite sex (heterosexual), or both sexes (bisexual)

target The person selected as the aim of an attack

transgender People whose characteristics or appearance do not match the physical gender to which they were born

verbal bullying Using words to hurt or gain power over someone

Index